Labrador Retrievers
Show Off

Sabrina Lakes

Sporting Dogs
FETCH
MASTERS
Show Off

xist Publishing

Check out all of the books in the Fetch Masters Series

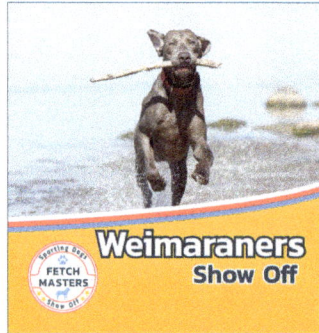

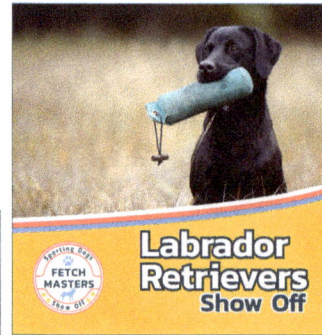

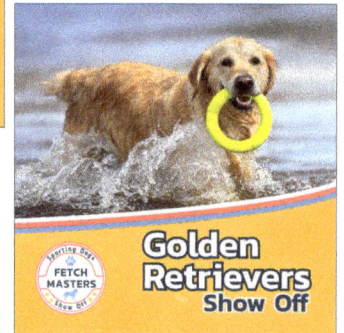

Cocker Spaniels Show Off

Weimaraners Show Off

Labrador Retrievers Show Off

Golden Retrievers Show Off

Published in the United States by Xist Publishing
www.xistpublishing.com
© 2025 Copyright Xist Publishing

First Edition
Hardcover ISBN: 978-1-5324-5527-8
Paperback ISBN: 978-1-5324-5528-5
eISBN: 978-1-5324-5526-1

PUBLISHED IN TEXAS

Table of Contents

Introduction to Labrador Retrievers

Labrador Retrievers, also known as Labs, are medium to large dogs. They have short, dense fur that is usually black, yellow, or chocolate. Labrador Retrievers come from Newfoundland, where they were bred to help fishermen. These dogs are friendly, loyal, and love to work and play. Labs are known for their strong swimming ability and gentle nature, making them excellent companions and sporting dogs.

Fun Facts About Labrador Retrievers

Labrador Retrievers are great swimmers. Their webbed feet and thick tail, called an "otter tail," help them move quickly through the water. Labs have strong noses that help them find things, which is why they are often used as search-and-rescue dogs. Labrador Retrievers are one of the most popular dog breeds in the world. They are loved for their playful and kind personalities.

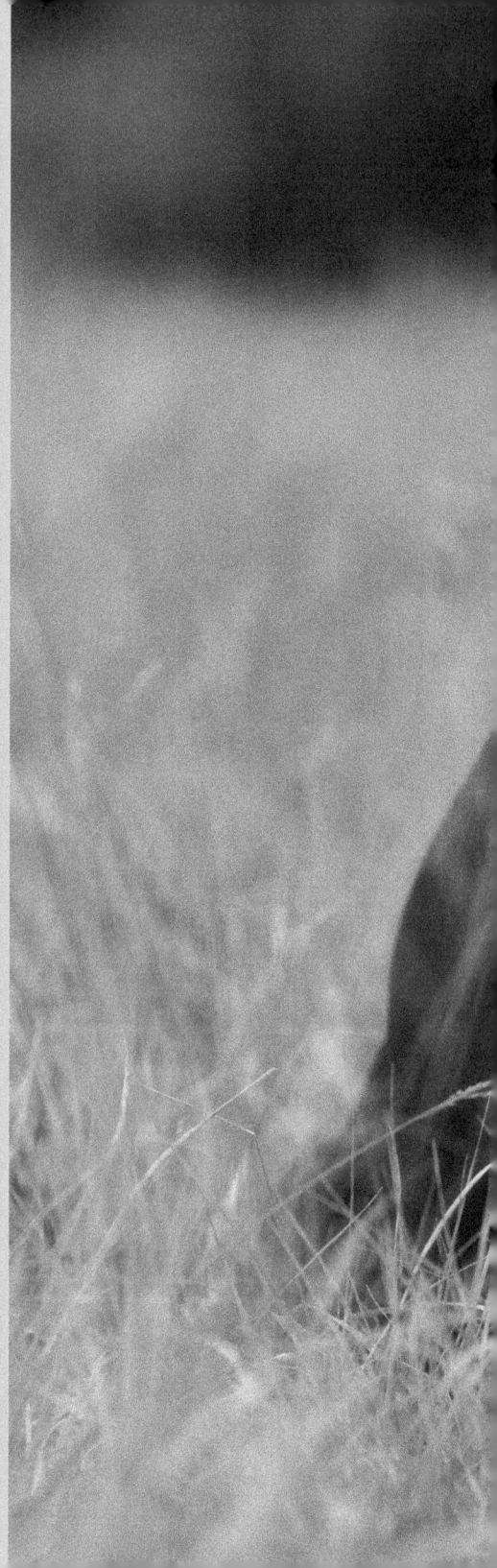

What is Sporting?

Sporting means helping hunters find and bring back animals. Labrador Retrievers are great at finding birds like ducks. They use their strong sense of smell and their love of water to track down and bring back the animals. Sporting dogs like Labs have a lot of energy and need to run, swim, and play every day.

Why Labrador Retrievers are Great Sporting Dogs

Labrador Retrievers are great sporting dogs because they are strong, smart, and love to work. They can run quickly on land and swim powerfully in the water. Their gentle mouths help them bring back birds without damaging them. Labs are friendly and work well with people, making them perfect for many sporting activities.

Training a Labrador Retriever

Training a Labrador Retriever is fun and rewarding. Start with simple commands like "sit," "stay," and "come." Use treats and praise to reward good behavior. Labs love to learn and respond well to positive training. Keep training sessions short and playful. Practicing every day helps your dog learn quickly.

Games to Help Labrador Retrievers Learn

Games are a great way to train Labrador Retrievers. Play fetch to teach them to bring things back. Hide treats around the house or yard for them to find. This helps them use their noses and stay focused. You can also play "find the toy," hiding their favorite toy and letting them search for it. These games keep Labs active and happy.

A Day in the Life of a Sporting Labrador Retriever

Labrador Retrievers start their day full of energy. After breakfast, they are ready to work. They join hunters in fields or near water, using their noses to find birds. Labrador Retrievers are fast and can swim through lakes, ponds, or streams to find what they are looking for. They love being outdoors and helping others.

Working with the Team

Labrador Retrievers work well with hunters and other dogs. They stay focused on finding and bringing back animals. When they find a bird, they gently carry it back without damaging it. Labs are proud of their work and always do their best to help their team.

Caring for a Labrador Retriever

Labrador Retrievers need healthy food to keep their energy high. They eat twice a day to stay strong. Grooming a Lab is easy because their short fur only needs brushing a few times a week. Regular grooming helps keep their coat shiny and clean. Labs also need their nails trimmed to stay comfortable.

Keeping Your Labrador Retriever Healthy

Exercise is very important for Labrador Retrievers. They love to run, play, and swim every day. Regular walks and playtime help them stay happy and fit. Regular check-ups with the vet are also important to keep your Lab healthy. These dogs love to be active and spend time with their families.

Labrador Retrievers at Rest

After working or playing hard, Labrador Retrievers need time to rest. They enjoy naps in cozy spots and like to be close to their families. Rest helps them get ready for the next day. Labrador Retrievers are happiest when they are around their loved ones.

Fun Activities for Labrador Retrievers

Labrador Retrievers enjoy playing even when they are resting. They like toys that bounce, squeak, or float in water. Puzzle toys can keep their minds busy, and they enjoy spending time with their family. Labs are loyal, loving dogs who always bring joy to those around them.

Glossary

Birds   Small game that Labrador Retrievers help hunters find.

Breeds   Different types of dogs, like Labrador Retrievers.

Commands   Words used to tell a dog what to do, like "sit" or "stay."

Exercise   Activities like running, swimming, or playing to keep dogs healthy.

Fetch   A game where a dog brings back a thrown object.

Grooming   Caring for a dog's coat, ears, and nails to keep them clean.

Hunting   An activity where dogs help find and bring back birds or animals.

Sporting Dogs   Dogs that help hunters find and bring back animals.

Webbed Feet   Feet with skin between the toes that help dogs swim better.

Index

Keyword List

Nouns	Verbs	Adjectives	Adverbs
bird	bring	active	actively
breed	carry	alert	eagerly
coat	chase	bright	easily
command	eat	friendly	excitedly
dog	find	gentle	gently
ears	fetch	happy	happily
exercise	groom	hardworking	quickly
family	guide	healthy	safely
fetch	help	large	strongly
fur	hide	loyal	well
game	learn	playful	
hunter	play	proud	
Labrador	retrieve	quick	
nose	run	smart	
scent	search	strong	
tail	sniff	swimming	
team	swim	thick	
treat	train	trained	
vet	work	wet	
water	rest	working	

28

Sporting Dogs

FETCH
MASTERS

Show Off

www.ingramcontent.com/pod-product-compliance
Lightning Source LLC
LaVergne TN
LVHW070835080426
835508LV00031B/3472